TRIAGE

TRIAGE

poems

Renée Rossi

LOST HORSE PRESS
Sandpoint, Idaho

ACKNOWLEDGMENTS

2007 Best of the Net Anthology: "Movements"
*Body Language: Poems of the Medical Experience (*BOA Editions): "Unnamable
   Galaxies" and "Loving, Meticulously"
Comstock Review: "Still Life"
di-verse-city: The Austin International Poetry Festival Anthology: "Potato" and "A
   Letter"
Hospital Drive: "Consent for a Laryngectomy"
Ilya's Honey: "The Golden Ratio"
Journal of Medical Humanities: "The Green Flash"
Locus Point: "Gross Anatomy" and "Shock Collars"
Sentence: "A Sonnet of Statements" and "Compassion"
Sojourn: "Stone Beds"
Southwestern American Literature: "A Malnourished Boy Asks for a Dictionary"
   and "It Grabs Me"
Tuesday: An Art Project: "Jaw Cancer Pastoral"

To my family, friends, fellow poets, and mentors—my gratitude for your support
and generosity. A special thanks to Donna Moore-Ede for always believing in me.
Thank you, dear Nance Van Winckel and Jorge Roby Misium for your close reading,
invaluable criticism, and help in assembling this manuscript. My deepest gratitude to
the many people who have allowed me into their lives, and who appear in these poems.

Cover Art by Renée Rossi, *Cell-Portrait #3,* 14 x 10" watercolor, detail.
Author photo by Gail Nogle.
Book & Cover Design: Christine Holbert.

FIRST EDITION

This and other fine LOST HORSE PRESS titles may be viewed online at
www.losthorsepress.org.

LIBRARY OF CONGRESS CATALOGING-IN-PUBLICATION DATA

DataNames: Rossi, Renee, author.
Title: Triage : poems / by Renee Rossi.
Description: First edition. | Sandpoint, Idaho : Lost Horse Press, 2016.
Identifiers: LCCN 2015049922 | ISBN 9780990819387 (alk. paper)
Classification: LCC PS3618.O8526 A6 2016 | DDC 811/.6—dc23
LC record available at http://lccn.loc.gov/2015049922

To my parents, who showed me how to survive

TABLE OF CONTENTS

I ZIP UP MY PARKA

I drive to the restaurant where you used to eat, where you didn't pay the bill. I'm late. Your crazy quilt purse sits on the seat beside me. The purse with all the stitches you mastered—blanket, feather, chain—for those three things you'd need in the next place.

Once you coaxed me to sit in the car as you drove down our old street in reverse. I jumped out by the flower shop on Morang. Just in time. You said I couldn't go where you were going anyway.

I come upon the women with badly pocked faces but the kind of smiles that negate the cold. They say they'll take me to you. We descend in elevators through permafrost deep into earth. They gown me in white. Through the glass I see you curled up, wearing your lace anklets. It's enough to see you sleeping, your hair returned to its golden color.

LOVING, METICULOUSLY

He's swallowed bedsprings, screws, batteries,
coins, and most of a band radio.
All but his brains have been extracted.
The warden puts him in a cell with a blanket,
four walls and a light bulb swinging from a wire.
The light hypnotizes him into breaking it.
With the precision of a schoolboy arranging marbles,
he covers the shards with bits of gum, feasts

on Wrigley-coated glass, his ruse d'etre,
followed by a bumpy, windowless ride to the ER,
hands and ankles cuffed.
The gowning and blood-letting and probing
make him feel alive again.
Counting backwards by 7s, he skips 86
sinking under an ether halo.
Look at us in our white coats

labeled with degrees, thinking we can
save what he cares about least. I peer
down a long tube into his darkness—
surrogate mother surgeon plucking glass
from his insides. He is the living anatomy
teaching me to love, meticulously.

THE GOLDEN RATIO

It was right after the chicken flew over the fence and somebody ran to rescue her from the neighbor's dog that the rats found their way into the coop. It was something about music filtering through the house and how my fingers raked over the treble strings as if there were lightning in the air and it charged them with luminosity. I am not afraid of the dark. I walked early this morning under a thousand brilliant stars. Their beauty maimed me. My father holding his coffee cup and whistling his breath out the way he always did. There is always trepidation in the universe, a speckled snail shell coiling its Fibonacci spirals *in extremis*. The snails have suffered and you have suffered all but weightlessness and coronas. I have a place in the sky where the noises don't suffer. A woman under the Albuquerque blue said that those were not contrails, but chemtrails and we were under siege. Walking in weighted circles, I find that my metacarpal to first phalanx ratio is the same as yours, which inspires black-cut silence and violent threads of rain, and I want to step out of this landscape for a moment so as to come back slightly more infinite.

MOVEMENTS

I

I walk on a trembling cave bridge
underground. Eyeless fish swim beneath me.

Fish happy never to surface
completely. Removing a bandage

from an amputee, I see maggots crawl out
over his stump. Only I can feel them. He stands
on his other leg and loses his bladder on me.
Only now I feel the warmth trickling down
my own leg. His eyes wet. In this recurring dream

I'm inside my old house exploring
new rooms added since I've left.
Through large windows, people look into my bedroom.
I'm part of the old surgical theater, etherized,
counting backwards,
a tinny blood taste on my tongue.

Yet I remain in this house when they lift
its sagging foundation, sighing and creaking.

II

I touch people

without my gloves on,
without a mask. I breathe them. At autopsy,

I hold the calcified heart of a young child. Inside
the heart is an eggshell. Inside
the eggshell a little bird.

III

Is that the same child
who asked me if
there are bones in heaven?

DOG DAYS: DETROIT

I used to ride my bike down the sidewalk with my eyes closed to see how far I'd go before hitting something. Nights, the police helicopter beamed its lights on the Harvey house until people filed out like fire ants from an angry mound. Dutch elms filtered sunlight over the street, roots pushing up cement into a cracked quilt. There were no explanations, simply a fan burning in the open window and me watching it suck the curtains into its vortex as my neighbor ran circles around the car that had crushed her dog in the drive.

MORTADELLA

: the name of the white-checkered ball of meat
we used to bounce off the deli cooler walls
where I worked as a clerk. I didn't know a sentient being
had been slaughtered, chopped, and reassembled.

One night you told me the cows huddled together and cried
in the field near your cement block house
because they knew they were going to slaughter
and I remember how intently I worked to save my fingers

at the meat slicer, never turning my back, never
answering a question even if the customer chided me
to *slice it thinner,* to make more out of the half-a-pound.
I was still a half-woman trying to work my way out

even if I handled meat and tongue and all
the forms of animals I would one day identify.
Mortadella sounded to me like *morte bella,*
        the beautiful death.

THE PRECISE MOMENT I DECIDE
TO SEEK LICENSE TO HEAL OTHERS

I must have been ten or so sitting in the waiting room of Detroit's
ER with my painful gums swollen over the edge of my teeth, some
viral exanthema of childhood, when the older lady with blue hair
walks out from the other side of the swinging door wringing her
hands and sits down next to me, saying her husband has water on
the brain. *They're giving him something to take the water away
and he's gonna hafta stay.* I'd been thinking a lot about the brain,
flipping through those acetate-layered anatomy books. That large
hulk of grey matter with its gyri and sulci I've imagined floating
in a little green algae pond inside a cave. And this lady is still
wringing her hands saying, *I only wish our life could go back to
the way it was.* Like my own grandmother, she doesn't know how
to drive a car or balance a checkbook. I imagine her tethers, her
I can'ts swelling up to hydrocephalus featured in the big books.
All her years of making beef bourguignon, glazed carrots, and
upside-down cake don't mean a thing here now. A month later I
teach my grandmother, turning sixty, to ride my pink Sears lady
bike with its dropped crossbar. At first she falls and falls but
finally rides away, hair neatly sprayed into place.

GROSS ANATOMY

There's something in the spleen of a so-called brain
that prefers to sate itself on stories

of lost sandwiches found in the folds of
four-hundred pound women or the man

with cockroaches nesting in a hole
in his face, how he droppered

alcohol in his ears to keep babies from bouncing
on the trampoline of his eardrum. There will always be

a creep dressed in her own language,
a cretin in satin, puttering

in a white coat and holding a tongue depressor,
wearing long, white gloves. A lady once

brought me a Mason jar filled with a year's worth
of dried mucus from her nose and mouth.

See the little flecks of red, she said, that's
what I really wanted to show you.

The spittle dried up and rolled around
like little rocks. I saved it.

OVENS MOUTH

The man could still speak but wrote on a tablet. His second wife would wring her hands outside the door to his room saying she could not take care of him at home. Honest enough to say she hadn't bargained for this, only married seven years, too early for this.

Darkness is long and narrow, low tide in Ovens Mouth, the skimmer skipping across the water, the muck and waves slapping. I feel waves pounding the rock in this little tear-stained cabin of pine walls. Nearby, grandfather's primitive duck decoys and a fog that wraps around every tendril of hair to silence the birds.

As the cancer eroded his jaw, it would work its way into the rich blood supply and let loose a gusher which couldn't be controlled at home. This became more frequent and there was little to do other than palliative care: cauterizing the little bleeders. Over and over again.

A thousand pieces of driftwood. I go down to the ocean and find the perfect piece of smooth granite lined with quartz for my son because the days ahead will be hard and he will need the strength of the stone and I will need the strength of a mother who goes to the post office and wraps a stone in tissue paper to send to her son in a box.

It is hard not to judge her as her husband lay there in pain, drooling and aware, the rest of his body not yet ravaged by the cancer. She is dressed to the nines: high heels, highly coiffed hair, a facelift, jewels and a heavy perfume that almost overpowers the scent of necrotic, dead tissue emanating from her husband's jaw.

My great-aunt collected glass transformer covers: blue, clear, green. They sit on the sill above the cabin window. She is long dead and so is the black walnut outside her old home on the lake. Wind, waves, the blue glare of TVs at night. The red and white striped awning of the Ebb Tide Restaurant is reflected in its glass windows.

The man comes back over and over into the hospital for his bleeding. He writes one day on his tablet that he's wealthy and he's just written her out of his will and will not tell her.

The chipmunk scurries under the old shed. You can't find him in Texas, hundreds of miles from here, my son wrapped in a new world, swaddled by his newfound aloneness. I am alone, a mother who has given her son to the world, swaddling her womb to close the empty space.

For days, the fog hangs in the trees like a ghost. The lobstermen's conversations echo over a thousand pieces of driftwood.

CLEAN-CONTAMINATED

Where coyote howls bend the moon,
where a cottonmouth slides into the river.

When oboes play, when your mother crawls
for her last Percocet. I was a mother

once, I loved all their wounds.

I painted them in iodine.

TOUGH LITTLE BEAUTY

In front of her cabin, rocks rely on the lake,
gulls rely on the lake, and skies stay interminably
grey. Here, under partial shade
of cedar, hemlock, evergreen,
at margins of limestone gravel and cobble beach
grows the tough little beauty,
the dwarf lake *Iris lacustris*,
from which one learns
fragility is situational—some,

but not too much sunlight. And disturbance—
wave action, ice scouring,
                              blowing sand.

Trabecular bone, potash, chemical smell . . .

          How do they know at crematoriums
          where one person ends and the next begins?

The clay mask she wore. The cracked mask. Her
          sapphires and opals.
Once, she made a path of stones to the garage.
Buddhists say nothing is ever stable—

not even the imprint of a memory,
not even the sparkle and hardness
of gems. Her painted landscapes
          summer   winter   fall   spring

Her last six years alone except for the cat asleep
on her bed. Except for a wind that blows moss
off rocks. Except for rain over eons
burning holes in limestone. Except for
the cranberry bog where
her canoe slumps under a tamarack.

The lighthouse blinks,
a freighter sounds its foghorns,
and the islands rumble.
            Dry ash trails in the wind.

Slowly, so slowly,
her right hand turns cold and blue
as if left out of her glove
one long winter night.

Between dictionary pages dried
cinquefoil and coreopsis call back
an afternoon spent lying on sun-heated glacial boulders.
The waves have their ways
of wearing down callous, of forcing loons' cries
            from somewhere behind red-rimmed eyes.

Ninety-five years—she watched stars—
dead then, dead now.

Dirt floor, old Frigidaire,
a clump of red-tipped tail fur
among pine needles, and the cabin
another year closer to the ground.

Birch fungus, cedar bough,
our stars, our decay.

Stone towers built deep
in the woods, in places
she'd never find again.

AT THE OASIS HOTEL

A monkey chained to a banyan tree points to his neck and then at the sky. A little girl tries to take his picture but he turns his head away. The feeling is a bald parrot who cries *hola hola*. Yet when you try to shake it, bright orange wings spread as if the fountain still had water, as if the man with the machete might stop his teeth from falling out.

ANATOMY OF A WOMAN

Her lungs are pink as baby flesh
barely stippled by carbon or city air,
lips not quite the right shade of vermilion.
She checked off the square,
donated what she was to what is—
eye sockets pinched empty

for their precious corneas. I can stare
all I want. Yet I still look away
nervously unsheathing
scalpels, unready
to peel her like an orange,
and she, more eyeless each day, greets
me. This once woman sealed with fixative.

How did she hold her first baby
in the crook of that stiffened arm?
Is she a mother, reconstituted
with a spray of Chanel?

I've opened *Gray's* to "abdomen."
Rectus abdominis is three times as wide cranially
where it is fleshy, as it is caudally,
where it is tendinous.

When I close my eyes I think I see her
chest rising with each breath. How
these carved scraps thud against the metal pail.

MARAÑÓNE

On the road you pass a rat hanging by a rope from a tree. In this land of strange trees, a certain sameness seizes you. It is not a peach, though you cradle it like one with your myopic eyes against the *cielo,* sky-heaven over the Gulf of Fonseca.

When you return, he's left you the same palm-sized bright orange fruit with the little drupe hanging from it. Embryo of the world.

And you know what his mother meant when she said he rattled the house, he shook curtains from the windows. *Marañóne* rolls off his tongue as you grab your Spanish dictionary. Cashew.

At night, men with machetes roll up in blankets, guard the makeshift clinic scabbed dogs and hens walk through by day. Dilantin hasn't yet cured the boy's seizures so his mother will rub a chicken egg over his body to remove the curse.

EX-VOTOS

He shows me a photo where a young woman holds a teacup
between her wrists. She
whose hands and feet he had to cut off

as gangrene set in. In the hospital,
I see a refrigerator with the sign:
no limbs on the lower shelf, please.

The lower shelf must be for memory—

as the universe carries this world
balanced gently between its wrists.

IN THE MUSEUM OF LOST MINERS

In Jerome, Arizona
doors still open into the hills
where pneumatic drills drove through rock and lung

and ghosts are toothless, sleeping
soundly as babies on their acre
of bones. We're told smelting coke
came from Wales, traveling the last sixty
miles by pack mule.

Azurite and malachite. All those fluorescing
rocks for which my boys keep pushing buttons

while I seek out underground gems
and granite kisses and girls in copper
dresses that spark sunset fires.

CHÁ HIBISCUS

The store in Chuy, Brazil where I bought the hibiscus tea bags had posters of women clad in skimpy bathing suits high on its walls like the hardware stores of my youth. We were always silent when my mother napped on hot afternoons as a window fan sang a serrated song. My kids will remember my shelf of different teas, dried petals, and leaves. They will call me a *curandera*. I have never checked to see if teabags fit into matchboxes, like Giacometti's tiny metal men did during the war. The years we take to reduce things. The hibiscus box is pink and holds ten small sacks of crushed calyces that turn deep crimson or magenta when infused with water. Not even, not ever the same color as blood.

SPARE PERFECTION

I'd seen women like you. We opened them
in medical school. Miliary disease,

little millet seeds, remnants of your ovaries.
Like buckshot, the professors said,

scattered everywhere. No, I thought it finer—
tatted lace or a rime of frost coating,

coalescing and freezing solid, draping
your insides. The text describes your ovaries

as *almond-shaped, pitted and scarred*
from the stigmata of ovulation. You say

your ovaries are your stigmata, source of all
your pain and joy. Clouds parting one day

to let you pass through, the bilious green
of your withered frame falling to earth.

I wipe your mouth one last time as I would
a child's. You close your eyes on the distillate

of yourself, a ten-pound box of ash and bone
reduced to earth's spare perfection I save.

HOUSE CALL

There is a table in the corner with small bags of roots and a tiny porcelain tea cup. A sleepy child stares from the hammock. On the adobe wall, a framed picture of a young woman with a thick, dark braid hanging down her back. *La vieja* is strong, with a shredded rag wrapped around her head. You see the opacity in her pupils, her swollen foot painted in gentian violet made from the roots. When she shows you her kitchen with its piñon-burning stove and blackened holes in the wall, her smile is papaya.

MONAHAN'S RESTAURANT NEXT TO A MOTEL ON JEFFERSON: DETROIT, CIRCA 1974

whores leaking mascara
faces painted to the jaw lines
winter's fur over lace slips

formica tables with vinyl seats
seats that swivel
green order checks stabbed onto a spike

short orders
cinnamon rolls sliced and buttered and fried under a hood

a jukebox playing "You Can't Always Get What You Want"
hamburgers for breakfast sunny-side up

a glass-eyed busboy named Tonk who shuffles and
        is later shot on his front porch
glass windows
cash-only till

classifieds read on the corner stool every morning
        by a man misplaced from California

the smell of whiskey on Robert's breath
the smell of boiling potatoes in the back room
hash browns

rolled joints for tips
a stash in Della's hairnet
Della's daughter's scarred face after pressure cooker
        explosion cooking greens

front-zippered blue polyester smock with deep pockets
propositions while wearing dead great-grandfather's
     tarnished gold wedding band

rotten eggs saved for Devil's Night
two washes with lavender-scented shampoo to remove the grease

PAPER DOLLS

I release you, lighter than ice-wind, to old bone winter
as I once released cut-out paper dolls
from your second story window.

I release the women rocking in the halls,
their paper spines roped to chairs.
I release you from the plane

you once said you flew too close to the moon
but thought it best not to land against *the white of . . .*
bright white, almost blinding. I release you

from the weight of movement,
from the slow organic decay of my own fear
in following you.

IT GRABS ME

Though his shelves are now empty of medicine, if they pay five *lempiras,* the fat doctor will examine them for *parasitas.* Mother of God, says the *padre* from María Concepción as he pats his belly. Mother of God, says the Lenca woman who finally finished nursing her four youngest. It is still the wet season, still the days of hookworms wading into soles of shoeless feet, grabbing on between the toes. I see the pale blue hand-stitching in her neckline as I listen to her lungs: the rattle of empty acacia pods. *Madre de Dios.* She walks away barefoot like the leaf-cutter ant, carting all she owns on her head.

POTATO

I pulled a large weed growing through the mint marigold.
        The tuber surprised me
growing in the composted scraps,
white and bare as a bald head with strands of earth stuck to it
while my son played a sonatina in the house,
and I remembered the woman who screamed as she labored
in the hospital where he was born
        as if she were dying,
how I took the epidural to ease my childbirth, my remorse
at having taken the easy way

but, still, I have this scar across my abdomen
from my son playing a sonatina as if it were a bird
singing through the walls. *They all scream like that,*
        the nurses said.

After my mother died, my father played a recording of a loon,
low and sonorous, over and over. The loon,
        its eyes red, always mourning.
Yet, how perfect this potato with three eyes and tubers
growing around it. How imperfect is the compost of memory,
dark, teeming, in its soul-raking of
birth, death, the transit of time between.

The metronome paces the sonatina's eighth notes
and I once screamed for morphine, screamed to make it easier,
as another woman screamed because she wanted the pain,
because pain, she believed, would purify.

I replant this potato, thankful for a world
that brings me scraps of eggshell and caterpillar,
classical sonatinas under perfectly formed fingers,
and flight of the common loon under a northern sun,
the loon so named for its clumsiness on land,
    and the potato, so white,
so earthly, so unexpected.

FAMINE

I

In Ireland 1847 during the great potato famine,
they found the couple frozen, dead from starvation,
in a deserted cabin, where he'd tried to warm her. He carried her
when she had the fever, and when he could walk no farther,
he held her freezing feet against his chest. And
that is how they died.

II

It is not simple, this lightning crackling, the smell of petunias,
and the wood turner in his shop saying, Yes, maple is denser than
cherry, the grain lines need to be felt. There is a pink beyond
the clouds, and not the words she is a mess, she is anxious.
If I stay with her, I will die. If I stay with her,
I will not carry her.

HOME PASTORAL

My husband   his white toes in the bath   his white toes
all the thin little scars   riding over   one body
          the sun gnawing my skull   an empty gourd

he studies rhomboids   cleans the metal grates
the lifeless windowpane   of a framed yard
the bird that flew   into our window   broke its neck

we stand halfway   to our mouths   his gullet
spills our seeds   we have chosen
          not to live aware of   the hyacinth bean vine

with its purple pods   all good   intentions
dropping to earth   gnaw little heart
for it is bitter   I am here   heartbeat

a pigeon crying out loud   this thin   sun aching
behind a cloud   a postage stamp
          marked airmail   for joy

MURDER CITY

Go a little faster, father, cars are passing us. It was his default to drive as if he were still the cop on patrol in his cruiser. It was our default to call him a *pig* when we were angry with him because that's what everyone in Detroit called the cops.

I had a baby once and put her in a balloon basket and threw a stone over the edge. She had blond curls and was last seen somewhere near a bruise on the moon. Maybe I inflated helium balloons and tied them to my lawn chair, flying up over Murder City's air space to fetch her. Maybe the smell of rosemary brought us back to a basement kitchen where a woman floured herself up to her elbows and leaned into a rolling pin.

An everlasting, foamy glass of amber never settles to the harmonic frequency of the Magnavox cranking tunes beside it. My father, who used to sleep with his gun, steps outside with ice-cold beer in hand and flips steaks on the grill as he listens to Mario Lanza belt operas. Here is the sweetness of bass and burning flesh, so large in memory but ever nearing its vanishing point on the horizon.

STILL LIFE

I

You said you'd paint me in a picture,
you, the woman in a bird cage
who grows smaller with each breath
who, now, is the tiniest voice.

The last tube of your paint is filled with air.

Listen to the bird thrashing
in your caged lungs,
flying out in gasps—

little cardinal that lands on my feeder today,
wrap your thin, red wings
around my still-life heart.

II

I slip the sapphire, the diamonds, the opal
off your blue fingers
bent at the tips, pointing
to the road in your oil painting.

Still life can be painted from your mind.
You said you'd just be
going for a little walk in the forest—

III

The last time we drove out to the country
it was winter and every barn was your grandmother's.
We looked for a sign—

the wild turkeys, the buck who stepped out
in front of the car, a barn owl searching

for mice. Someone had a small fire going
at the lake's edge where children warmed
their hands. Red-eyed children.

You said she made you sandwiches once
and placed them under the wagon seat.

I follow prints in the snow, the lake
iced over. You're melting now . . .

Little seeds in my pockets—

they will germinate
in the lint of this coming year.

BETWEEN TWO DOCTORS

That day you sent me pictures of a severed leg, even the patella
sitting correctly between the femur and tibia on blue drapes. Near
neatly stacked snap clamps. No, not many speak the language of
amputation, coil and recoil like the tubing on your back table. A
woman lies there out of view, out of the picture, she who will go
on living legless. And you have sewed over her stump. I wouldn't
have thought it like this.

Once, I took pictures of the sky above the Mackinac Bridge
until finally the spires were out of view and all that was left
was a memory of bridge. The clouds moved by as they do over
mountains, collecting air and water. I didn't want us to be the
spires that were left, nor the sun blocked by clouds, nor the water
moving away. But this woman, you said, she spent years injecting
herself with some prescription drug until the skin fell away from
her leg. And everything left between us was severed in that split
moment when the saw hit the bone.

THE GREEN FLASH

You walk in on a woman whose brain won't fit
back into her skull: her frontal lobes cut out
to fit this puzzle, to make the pieces fit.
There's a certain violence in holding a woman's hand

when you know she's going to die &
she doesn't know your third eye already
sees the mushroom cloud. That night you
sleep in grey woolens, dream you're

in Antarctica at dusk, seeing the elusive
green flash of the sun just before it drops below
earth. It must be a place where the air is clear
enough for the sun's camera to take

that instantaneous photo of you child-
like on the horizon and not knowing the head
is always shaved first before sterile
procedures involving the brain. Only

wishing you could go back to
that brightness, as when the hair you'd
gathered from your brush and placed gently around the yard
you found woven into a bird's nest the next day.

The last faces she sees must be grainy
little storm clouds passing across her pupils.
One of them is yours.
The hallways and corridors appear longer this night,

particles of silence and drifting dust motes.
As you drive home on the lighted highway
you meet her once again,
flashing past in the anxious cars.

COOKED EARTH

When my husband left, I had dreams of large feats—
trying to teach others how to fly and failing

because I didn't know how to fly. I would see
the little bird in me soar into a stone sky

and I'd scream white epithets from my dry
vocal cords. Screams no one could hear.

Somehow, the quaintness of things became proportional
to my grief, which the Ayurvedic teachings say

is stored in the heart, the lungs, the hips,
and god, where isn't it stored?

Learning Italian, I was stunned to know
terra cotta simply meant cooked earth.

All those years I'd managed to plant Jupiter's beard,
petunias and foxglove in terra cotta planters

thinking only *clay pot*. And how do passion vines, alive
so many winters, crash land in the first ground freeze?

UNNAMABLE GALAXIES

He grabs a model airplane kit
from the O.T.
inhaling its glue
then runs screaming
half-naked down the street,
two orderlies in pursuit.
They wrestle him down,
apply the straitjacket,
then pump a syringe full
of inertia into his thigh.
We are light-years away, watching

his centrifuge of human mind
slowly spin down
into the reality of its DNA
at the bottom of some test tube.
When the sine wave of reason
reaches its nadir, he crawls
into his black hole
and remains there.

His father once tried to beat,
then shame it out of him
as a watch ticked
next to his ear on a bedside table.
He turned to face the wall.
We were light-years away.

A MALNOURISHED BOY
ASKS FOR A DICTIONARY

Under early morning stars at San Marcos, roosters crow from the trees. A woman with fourteen children fell out of a tree trying to get her rooster down. It wanted to escape the iguanas.

You would feed the iguanas here, even if they bite your hands. You would feed them Spanish-English dictionaries because they, like *la gente,* really want to learn. The pages would rain as cassava and plantains from the bluest sky.

A little boy here already knows one English word—*toy.* It drops from his mouth like a tinkling bell, rolls down the dusty hillside.

CURTAINS OF WORDS

They kept adding to the volumes
names they couldn't use anymore,
names for sadness and despair,
names for the plight of orphans.

They kept reading lines that transformed
hope into a shallow peach
that wouldn't separate from its pit

Yet for all the dangling metal curtains of words,
a boy captured lovely zeroes in his mouth
and held them like a promise
that no one would ever extract.

POSTCARD FROM SAN JOSE, HONDURAS

I must tell you the way she paints
the *mestizo* Virgin Mary on a matchbox—

to earn a few *lempiras* for threadbare cotton dresses
and how the sun outlines her muscled
thighs against her legs heavily veined

from nine pregnancies. On the mat I see her, grieving
the buried placentas, the ones I empty my suitcase for.

I am here to palpate the abdomen, to touch
the flat and sunken shape. How do I

empty my suitcase as if I were not
Doctora gringa with my flat word *abdomen*
but this mother living? You ask me, is she still living

in that packing crate with her three children
Nunca, Nada, & Shhhh? Yes,
they still run barefoot in the yards

hoping to catch a flying chicken.
And when she watches them, she has
this toothless smile as a butterfly

rash spreads across her face.
It's almost like praying to the Honduran sky
for the rain of fish to fall.

COMPASSION, 1987-1988

When Herr Doktor told us about the people he saw burning, the *Deutsches Jungvolk* look still lingered in his eyes. Then he'd tell the story of a 'stupid' mother who protected us from her donations to the gene pool by not following his directions for ear drops and killing her kid, or how the authorities should take all the fat women, particularly those who look like elephants, and cargo plane them back to Africa. He devised schemes for sterilization centers where mothers on Medicaid could walk through arches to zap their ovaries. We listened every morning in the Children's Cafeteria after rounds as we ate silently, filling in for the children he didn't have, for the youth he lost—we, bright-eyed, eager to learn, as easy to crush as he once was.

NEARNESS

The nearness of things preserves their farness,
the farness in being far preserves their nearness.

— *M. Heidegger*

My childhood was an open book
without any page markers—
a rock garden in one corner
of the yard, an old wine barrel spilling
strawberries from the sides,
a grocery sack left in the street
because it was too heavy to carry.

There are more angels than wounds
on earth. The nuns told me this.
And I believed the soul was a harp
you practiced on. Over and over.
Until the fingers grew callused,
and you parted taut strings
to climb down the vine.
A plough with copper blades and
sheaves of golden wheat awaited.

THE DAY OF DISSOLUTION

I decide to buy stamps of songbirds
with plumage and color, forever stamps

not flying toward any goals. I secure
twenty pink and black helium balloons,

and write words on them, release them
from the yard. My son blows out

twenty candles, one for each year,
without asking why. The cake is missing.

I try to pull some strings, gladiolas
bend from the weight. Here, the white

crepe myrtles drop petals as if there were
a wedding. I put on my wedding dress

and pogo-stick down the driveway, wave
good-bye to the train trailing on cement.

SHOCK COLLARS

Before I die, I would love to know the proper placement of salad and steak forks. The Chinese pistachio I've planted won't grow nuts and I'm afraid I'll never fall far from the tree. It's no sin to plant a weed garden. I've staked my spirit in the yard where stones are basted into the border. Our heavily implanted dogs don't stray far or they develop doggie permanents at the fenceless shock fence. Lonely perimeters are what we have. At the end, my grandfather stayed in a turn-of-the-century-home-for-the-elderly. The garage had a lazy Susan for the cars that couldn't go in reverse. Before they could back up. Before his mind stuck in reverse. Humble pie, he used to say. I could only feed him chocolates then. Such pleasure in his rheumy, vacuous eyes despite a spine contorted as a paper clip. A younger version of me sticks contact paper in cupboards and wears his dark-rimmed glasses. When I think about it, I'd rather be seduced in space than lost. The stars far outnumber the dust motes.

JAW CANCER PASTORAL

Slowly, a tractor digs a hole,
a bell rings like an injured squirrel

and a boy grinds two acorns
                to precise squares—
he throws them as one would dice

without numbers. Business as usual
                in shirtsleeves, tie,
vest, and polished leathers.

Between the fallen acorns and the oak,
                another injured man
puts his severed fingers on ice

                and marrow still drips,
drips from clouds in the sky above

Hamburg, above half-bombed out
Gothic churches and skyscrapers.

DETROIT, SIX DEGREES

I pray for the swirling snow wind to let up,
for the pine trees to straighten,
for the jet bridge to open. I understand
the poet saying *the tender gravity of sadness*
as if words carry the weight of snow

and an unfinished prison,
I-beams hammered to the sky.
Prisoners won't make it to this prison—
too many houses burned to the ground.
The weight of a prison is too much,
half-finished rooms exposed.
After every single window is broken,
may everything be left unfinished
rather than demolished or burned or boarded up.

Today, as ice on the Detroit River rises in sheets,
all the city's broken glass shoves ashore in protest.
Decay Detroit. In six degrees, smoke rises
from your stacks, burnt-out two-by-fours
are exposed in attics, a foot of white covers
your front yards' weeds and trash.

Motor City, I long ago stopped knowing you
as you settled into the next ancient city
lost for eons to be dug out later.
In our yard, we used to tamp the snow, spray it
with water, layer upon layer, to freeze
for an ice rink. Our nostrils froze as did
the city. There were no fires. The cold
made us reach inside to feel our hearts.

DREAM #2916

I am three legs and wobbly,
a few extra threads in my shawl. The warm
    something around my neck makes me laugh.

Pull a few teeth. A cockroach walks in and out
my ribcage: the fisherman has split
    me open

and only half-notes come tumbling out,
    heart sand and gypsum.

NECESSITY POEM

For the author who said he wrote from cellular memory about his father who had twelve surgeries. Did you see the last pope? He was hunched over and trached, he was the emblem of the dome. I have twelve surgeries in my knapsack.

He said you cut on people, you actually cut on people?

I said yes, with their permission, of course.

He said he was writing about torture—

was he interviewing torturers, I asked. I was one.

I live in a cellular space: it is bright green and it shines from its heart. There may be eggshells around this heart. I have two dogs and I skate around other people's sorrow. Outside, it is warm and a fountain dribbles and children throw balls. The background noise empties a truck on the street. My father told me once of a man who emptied a container truck and the forklift flipped on him.

Once, a woman who was young and eager walked into an operating room and an eyeball rolled across the floor to greet her.

There must be lavender in the air today and sandalwood to help ease memory.

There are metal rollers and a large lamppost and someone clips tiger lilies.

There is a fake candle in the room where flames are not allowed.

Thank you, thank you for making our mother's death so painless they said. Thank you for the narcotic that stilled the tooth nibbling at the soul of our deadening mother. I must have morphine on my breath. The mortar shell had engraved on it a poem before it blew up Sarajevo, or was the poem engraved after?

When the tube was pulled from the child's throat, the lining from his trachea was attached to it.

There are grackles here, not crows, and their cry is different.

I might have used a xister to avoid grief. It scrapes tissue from bone.

I was hurled into space once with my mother's ashes. A ten-pound box of ash and bone. A Chrysler New Yorker. Going seventy. My mother collected depression glass, thick-walled, blue and green. A little white moth flies around a woman's head. Celestial navigation. Truth is a heavy word much like celestial in its heavenly implications. I never wanted to hurt anyone.

There are no places here for phantom limb pain.

I remember bells that twinkled under his coat when he walked into a room.

I remember a man who bent back bare fig trees and covered them in burlap for winter.

But I want to avoid bringing in winter unless it carries the weight of snow.

Unless it carries something with it that will melt.

PRAYER FOR AN OPEN HEART

Having seen them cut open her heart. Having seen rose petals
    fall out
until the floor was covered in a fragrant heap

of dust. What rose bush dies in this world to create
such petals? Perhaps she swept leaves from her garage

or collected glass like my grandmother, who also died
in winter, the branches' bare arms and frozen pond

comforting her through the windows. All that grey snow
                       heaped up against the silence.

A SONNET OF STATEMENTS

in Ovid, the raped woman's tongue is cut out and slithers
caterpillar-like toward her destroyer

bonobos claim the whole spectrum of sexuality,
having sexual encounters every 1.7 hrs. in captivity

the smell of fresh bread in a bakery is mitigated
by the promise of baker's lung

people swell magnificently in wide hallways or
shrink in low-ceilinged rooms

all charisma is lost on life-sized inflatable Santas
on lawns at Christmas

don't use *to be* verbs: they clog the plumbing
worse than feminine hygiene products

in evolution, the day came when we put a thinking cap
on our reptilian brains

water drips through Breccia limestone where the earth's crust
acts as a cheesecloth sieve

eyeless fish without optic nerves swim underground rivers
in the Karst region

November's the bad month when warm water clashes
with cool air in the Great Lakes

a body in water temp below 92 degrees Centigrade
loses energy to its surroundings

Elizabeth Bishop left out solitude
from her Robinson Crusoe poem

the smoke bush has a plume of pale yellow spray
set against red leaves and is so named

many people flocked to see the hermit of Manana Island
who collected bits of grass for his sheep

AS IF LIGHTNING

Because I had a fish tank on a table I painted orange. Because I applied green flower decals to its edges so the fish would have something pleasant to look out at. Because I could walk the house with my eyes closed and know every detail intimately: the kitchen wall's charcoal-sketch of a woman holding a baby, the carved wooden ladle, the laundry chute from the bathroom to the basement, the little curtainless landing by the side door I had a fear of passing at night because someone could watch me. Because life seemed so brutally simple.

Lightning we watched summer afternoons from the Laing Street front porch, the one with the lattice work on the sides. During summer storms, drains opened for I-94 and street sewers overflowed, flooding our basement. A list of objects: dog food pellets expanding and sticking to the walls as the flood receded, an Underwood typewriter floating in the debris, the chairs upside down. In Eulogy: watermarks on cinder blocks and rolled-up, soaked carpets at the curbside. Because we lived in a small brick bungalow on Detroit's east side where Dutch elms lined the street. Because that canopy once stood proud.

A LETTER

Nothing changes with us.
Fresh water in the jugs.
A lovely rain.
Young girls drying their hair.
Stones stacked around the farm, some toppled
    and overrun with moss.
Venus scared by the new moon while stars founder in the sky.

And the sunsets, if you were here, copper and tin,
before the slow lighting of lanterns over the valley.

Still, the hunger looming,
impassable as a mountain.

STONE BEDS

I think I am only preparing a stone bed
as I move one of these old stones around to a new site
     in my garden
and the touch of Engadine dolomite takes me back to its scatter
at the shoreline bright white against green firs
and the lingering pink and orange sunsets:

my mother snapped Polaroids of us against that low-angled sun,
our large, shadowy heads bent forward as we
plucked stones one by one from the Great Lake shore
to build houses in the forest for whom, elves and fairies?
We lined their beds with dried cedar, used brightly-colored
     lichens for pillows,
broke the mushroom-shaped fungus off rotting paper birches
     and its white bark for bowls and plates
whole summer afternoons until the call of the dinner bell.

On these glacial moraines, islands strewn after the last ice age,
     the roads
crushed dolomite. A doe gave birth once on the gravel road
     in front of me,
a fawn unstable on its back legs hobbled away —
I retrieve it now as I do the limestone that rubbed
     my finger pads raw.

At three o'clock on a summer afternoon, the quarry blast sounded
close to where my great uncle fell asleep at the wheel and drove
     a train full of dolomite into the bay.
Hossack, he opened his garage once to show me the rafters
     lined with squirrel

tails, all orderly as the tools that hung on hooks.
He made a little golf course at the causeway out of stone, lifting
    his club to salute when a car passed by.
The Pointe had a large rock, too, with a tree growing out
    its center like saxifrage,
one that turned orange in the fall and shed its leaves on the rock.
    A lighthouse

blinked slower than the fireflies. Full moon nights we danced
against its reflection on the waves. Aurora borealis wrinkled lights,
    streamers across the already bright sky.

Under the stones, night crawlers we kept in large buckets
    of peat moss.
The occasional lady's slipper at the foot of an oak, delicate
    and confirming the need to build little houses in the forest.
Wild blueberries in August scattered the burnt floor
    of Cadogan's old growth forest. My grandmother brought
    her radio to scare off bears.
The unmistakable call of the red-winged blackbird at water's edge.
    The silver gleam of a pike's back in the reeds of the cove,
    long gone and fished out.

In the thirties before the causeway was put in, a Cherokee
brought in provisions for the old professor who wrote about
his winter alone on the island, the coldest of many. Ice breaking
and surging. How he caught the flu when he hadn't been around
a single soul in weeks. All this recorded in the *Weekly Wave*.

Many stones have holes dug out by acid after the last ice age.
I plant hens and chicks in them. A traveler of the northern
    woods leaves
foxfire to lead herself back home. No footprints,
just stone-lined paths in the forest.

HOW WE BECOME CLOSER
AS OUR CONTINENTS DRIFT APART

I held a thyroid gland
as big as a pulsing human heart
    while you kept your feet warm
against the wall all night.

A fire burned on the other side. The same day
you lifted a machete against a man
    I put a hole in a man's neck
so he could breathe.

BULL WITH BELLS, HONDURAS

I remember the way men dug trenches
to bring water from the mountains
to the village of *San Juan de las Lágrimas*.
The women huddled in front of
shacks with their children.

Why don't they stop making children
when there is no food, he asked.

The women would look right through you,
a dullness over their pupils. No rain,
no corn. Hammocks hung from the ceilings.

And the bus drove up the hillside, early
morning when the roosters jumped
from the trees. Guava and mango and papaya

women sold in bags on the highway.
¡And sometimes a cow fell off a cliff!

I ran through the village once
to find a sick man. Naked toddlers played
in pig shit. Yucca and banana

trailed the hillsides where baby chicks
walked. A schoolboy led a bull
up a steep path, its little bells shivering.

The villagers would sing at night
under the stars. They needed
new guitar strings. One night

we watched the full moon move
east to west across the low mountains.
There were no planes overhead,

only the satellites' darting
lights to remind us of
another world with cell phones

and fast cars and few children
who would name the trees.

DEAR ALIEN BLOSSOM

If there are flowers on any other planets,
they need reminders to open now.
I want to tell them that talking
doesn't move rosary beads.
I wanted to be saintly.
I should have been named Althea
because it's a crazy-lady name.
If I could be broken open, they would find
me full of rotary phone dials.
I want to tell the man next to me on the plane
to stop reading about 737 engines.
I saw him struggle with bar graphs,
little towers rising to the top of pages.
I want to tell him how
the clock's cuckoo still startles me
when it bolts through its doorway
after all these years.

TO AUTUMN

The cold snap chokes the chlorophyll
and plants die on the windowsill—
if only a pumpkin could outlive
frozen hands and harassing winds.
Blood turns to ice on the fountain's
warm-day wasps. Cider rots in the frig
as our fathers careen
into winter full bore without
their happy mansions and pensions
assured in the future's awkwardness.

It's all a fiction: how the baby boy
suckles at the breast. Yes, the fountains
dry, the pools empty and the gingko
leaves, if they didn't already know, fall at once
on a glory day. Nothing keeps pace.
There are no longer bridled horses.
The birds don't berate autumn.
Everyone wants to play a harp.
And our feet are tired. The long squall
and the energy of dragonflies simmering

over the fields. A leaf falls like it must.
The city wants its cars, its horns—
its crunching leaves are diadems
on the streets. What was once simple:
you must remember the childhood awe,
jumping into a raked pile of leaves, the way
the low sun blinds and cormorants head south

at the end of the day in V formation,
their long necks pointing their
heads to the final warmth.

IT ASKED A CRUMB OF ME

for Anne Lauterbach

I have a hole in my heart for gravity,
a pile of stones, the naked trees, broken stars . . .

all the prehistoric hooplas.
There really is a man who sees
pine siskins in his trees when it rains

hard on his trailer. I want
little existences, sneakers dangling from
oak limbs at the 45th parallel,

a homeless woman in New York City
who searches for stars in a dumpster
while a poet at the Met reads
Alice in Wasteland.

CONSENT FOR A LARYNGECTOMY

Loss of voice, loss of breathing through
    mouth, loss of sense

of smell and then the uncomfortable pause//
a tightening of my own glottis in response to//

a textbook opens its glossies in front of
my eyes, false cord strumming, epiglottis flapping.
    What does it look like

now? Your glottis is shaped like a star sucked into the night of . . .

what I want to do is let nature take
its rambling course into the Texas Panhandle

where the great Palo Duro Canyon's cut out
    slowly, little by little by a little
        river, Prairie Dog Town Fork,
the byproducts of combustion on human mucosa, bright red

Triassic shales, clay, and sandstone litter its rim with dysplasia,
    then carcinoma in situ,
the Trujillo and Tecovas yellow-pink and lavender shales,
    full-blown invasive finally the Ogalalla
sandstone, silt, and caliche, the whole of geologic history
in these bare canyon walls
    a substrata of damaged mucosa, too,

and what has this to do with loss of a larynx?
      You'll swallow just the same as before,
in fact, never again aspirating on

a cracker in your windpipe. In the usual sense, no, you will not
be able to swim. Water sucked straight into
the lungs. Summer, this landscape is desert-

like. Don't smell and taste go together? Bargaining
against the pleasure of years watching sunsets smoking Pall Malls
filterless. As protection against dust,
the trachea undergoes metaplasia to withstand the now

harsh environment, exposure for which you'll wear
a little apron over a bare hole in your neck. Not only
      water but wind

whipping through the canyons over years causes such erosion, too.
You'll drive for miles across the High Plains south of Amarillo,
flat, the treeless country inspiring

only drowsiness, mirages & so

forth, until you enter Palo Duro, overlook the rim of
      its eight-hundred foot abyss, at the bottom of which,
          a narrow ribbon of lush
cottonwood awaits you: the alternative, you ask—a slow suf-

focation though no one will
                describe that for you.

MEDITATION ON A SNAIL SHELL

I look at your snail shell spilling sand, speckled brother of the sea. And do I need to tell you the speckles dry up at the center just like stars in our galaxy? This morning the full moon hung in the sky like a lost lantern. And grackles swung in the air, hanging by their own violet-black threads. I've watched the sycamore lose leaves and reveal its olive-skinned bark so many autumns I'm merely atoms in the air around it. If I could tell you, my love, what type of tree you are, though, it's the bur oak, sometimes breaking off arms, sometimes unfolding. And your hands play songs off-key on an old piano with warped hammers in a country I've never seen. But it is still music.

BRUSHSTROKES AFTER CHAGALL'S
BOUQUET OF DREAMS

Your birds without theories
as clouds whirl above, little figurines

dancing over Vitebsk. How do you feel about
the way naked trees paw at skyscrapers

outside the museum? Gouache and pastel,
enough ink to lift a chalice to the sun.

God blended icons and threw dust
in our eyes. Because you draw a watermark

in our dreams, a round theater ceiling
playing for all corners of the earth.

•

Sun shines on silver buckets,
a man reads poetry to trees

while his brother taps them to find heartwood.
Maybe all along I cut on people

because I was afraid to heal myself:
scalpel, loupes, knots thrown of fast-

absorbing gut suture. So I could spill open
later. Arjuna bark stripped to heart tonic.

I will go deeper and strip bark from your insides,
pileated woodpecker. Pruning away.

Because I am not afraid of a man on a red ladder.
Is it enough to wear rubber boots?

.

You must stand with the headless figures, marching,
pad yatras, to the pits they will be buried in.

Cast clouds overhear absent birds
in a café, Muzak spilling into a courtyard.

I don't know when it began, but the man still taps on
the tree: a world of knots and broken limbs,

dreams shot clean through with red revelations,
half a sky away from sandhill cranes

and formations of animal glyphs, the smallest
creatures expelling what I want to tell you.

NOTES

"Tough Little Beauties":

The description of *Iris lacustris* in the first stanza derives from an essay in *Tough Little Beauties: Selected Essays & Other Writing* by Stephanie Mills.